Supporting Children with Depression to Understand and Celebrate Difference

The 'Get to Know Me' resources aim to support children, with those around them, who may have additional/special educational needs. They are designed to empower the professionals and adults who support those with identified needs. Developed by child psychologist Dr Louise Lightfoot, the series includes activities specific to anxiety, depression and Obsessive Compulsive Disorder (OCD). In supporting the social and emotional health of students, it equips them with the ability to thrive, personally and academically.

This book has been created for key adults (teachers, therapists and parents) as a complement to the picture book and draw along versions of *Silver Matilda* – a traditional narrative story exploring thoughts, feelings and sensations experienced by many children with depression.

The activities in this book offer practical tools and strategies to support the child and those around them, in addition to information specific to the condition to improve understanding of a child's needs to promote empathy and acceptance.

Picture book and draw along versions of *Silver Matilda* are available separately, and as part of the Get to Know Me: Depression set.

Dr Louise Lightfoot is an Educational and Child Psychologist working with children and young people aged 0–25. She holds a BA in Educational Studies, MEd in the Psychology of Education and doctorate in Educational and Child Psychology. Louise has worked in a variety of settings ranging from mainstream schools to secure units and psychiatric facilities, and has a special interest in working to empower at risk or 'hard to reach' groups. As a person who suffers with Ehlers Danlos, stroke and dyslexia, she has a first-hand understanding of the frustrations and difficulties that accompany a specific physical or learning difficulty. Louise currently works as an HCPC registered Independent Psychologist. If you would like to discuss working with her, please contact Louise at: louise.lightfoot@hotmail.co.uk.

Catherine Hicks is an East Yorkshire artist, illustrator, wife and mother. She spent 13 years as a Registered Veterinary Nurse before injury and chronic illnesses led to her creative hobby becoming therapy. When Catherine and Louise were introduced, it was obvious they were kindred spirits and from there the Get to Know Me Series was born.

GET TO KNOW ME SERIES

Series author: Dr Louise Lightfoot
Illustrated by: Catherine Hicks

The **'Get to Know Me'** series is a series of resources aimed at children with additional needs and the professionals who support them in the mainstream primary classroom. Each resource concentrates on a different condition and comprises of three titles, available separately.

A **traditional children's picture book** – designed to support the individual child but also to be used in whole class teaching, to encourage an empathetic and inclusive environment.

An **interactive work book**. This is a workbook version of the story in which indvidual children are encouraged to interact with the story in a creative way – through writing, drawing, scrap booking, collage, activities etc. (templates and cut outs will be made available online). Children are more likely to understand and process information if they have had to actively engage with it. The workbook will aid long-term recall and increase the level of understanding.

A **practitioner guide** created for key adults (teachers, therapists and parents) by a child psychologist, with activities specific to each condition. These activities will link to the books and offer practical tools and strategies to support the child and those around them in addition to the information specific to the condition to improve understanding of a child's needs to promote empathy and acceptance.

https://www.routledge.com/Get-To-Know-Me/book-series/GKM

Books included in this series:

Set 1 Get to Know Me: Anxiety
Available as a set and individual books

Book 1
Supporting Children with Anxiety to Understand and Celebrate Difference
A Get to Know Me Workbook and Guide for Parents and Practitioners
PB 978-0-8153-4941-9
eBook 978-1-351-16492-4

Book 2
Sammy Sloth
Get to Know Me: Anxiety
PB 978-0-8153-4953-2
eBook 978-1-351-16452-8

Book 3
Draw Along With Sammy Sloth
Get to Know Me: Anxiety

PB 978-0-8153-4942-6
eBook 978-1-351-16484-9

Set 2 Get to Know Me: Depression
Available as a set and individual books

Book 1
Supporting Children with Depression to Understand and Celebrate Difference
A Get to Know Me Workbook and Guide for Parents and Practitioners
PB 978-0-8153-4943-3
eBook 978-1-351-16480-1

Book 2
Silver Matilda
Get to Know Me: Depression
PB 978-0-8153-4945-7
eBook 978-1-351-16476-4

Book 3
Draw Along With Silver Matilda
Get to Know Me: Depression
PB 978-0-8153-4946-4
eBook 978-1-351-16472-6

Set 3 Get to Know Me: OCD
Available as a set and individual books

Book 1
Supporting Children with OCD to Understand and Celebrate Difference
A Get to Know Me Workbook and Guide for Parents and Practitioners
PB 978-0-8153-4948-8
eBook 978-1-351-16468-9

Book 2
Tidy Tim
Get to Know Me: OCD
PB 978-0-8153-4950-1
eBook 978-1-351-16460-3

Book 3
Draw Along With Tidy Tim
Get to Know Me: OCD
PB 978-0-8153-4951-8
eBook 978-1-351-16456-6

Supporting Children with Depression to Understand and Celebrate Difference

A Get to Know Me Workbook and Guide for Parents and Practitioners

Dr Louise Lightfoot

Illustrated by Catherine Hicks

LONDON AND NEW YORK

First published 2020
by Routledge
2 Park Square, Milton Park, Abingdon, Oxon OX14 4RN

and by Routledge
52 Vanderbilt Avenue, New York, NY 10017

Routledge is an imprint of the Taylor & Francis Group, an informa business

© 2020 Dr Louise Lightfoot & Catherine Hicks

The right of Dr Louise Lightfoot and Catherine Hicks to be identified as authors of this work has been asserted by them in accordance with sections 77 and 78 of the Copyright, Designs and Patents Act 1988.

All rights reserved. The purchase of this copyright material confers the right on the purchasing institution to photocopy or download pages which bear either the photocopy or eResources icon and a copyright line at the bottom of the page. No other parts of this book may be reprinted or reproduced or utilised in any form or by any electronic, mechanical, or other means, now known or hereafter invented, including photocopying and recording, or in any information storage or retrieval system, without permission in writing from the publishers.

Trademark notice: Product or corporate names may be trademarks or registered trademarks, and are used only for identification and explanation without intent to infringe.

British Library Cataloguing-in-Publication Data
A catalogue record for this book is available from the British Library

Library of Congress Cataloging-in-Publication Data
A catalog record has been requested for this book

ISBN: 978-0-8153-4943-3 (pbk)
ISBN: 978-1-351-16480-1 (ebk)

Typeset in Avant Garde Gothic Std
by Apex CoVantage, LLC

Visit the eResources: www.routledge.com/9780815349433

Contents

	Acknowledgements	viii
	Introduction to the Resource Pack	x
CHAPTER 1	Feelings generator	1
CHAPTER 2	Sympathy or empathy	7
CHAPTER 3	Using puppets and play to explore emotions	11
CHAPTER 4	True or false	15
CHAPTER 5	Miracle questions	19
CHAPTER 6	Colour your feelings	23
CHAPTER 7	Compliment cards, part 1	27
CHAPTER 8	Compliment cards, part 2	31
CHAPTER 9	Remember a time	35
CHAPTER 10	Always, never, everybody	39
CHAPTER 11	Feelings sorter	43
CHAPTER 12	The bridge to success	47
CHAPTER 13	Silver Matilda's Activity Book	51
CHAPTER 14	Silver Matilda's Board Game	69
CHAPTER 15	What happens next?	75
CHAPTER 16	Alternate ending?	79

Acknowledgements

To Katrina my editor, thank you for taking a chance and sticking with us, especially during our particularly 'imperfectly flawed' moments! You have been a wonderful source of personal support and a professional wisdom.

Professor Kevin Woods for your (I often wondered if misguided) belief in me and continued support. Here's to being a square peg in a round hole.

The University of Manchester and the students of the Doctorate of Educational Psychology Course, in particular Jill and Ben Simpson, for their collaboration, perspective and belief.

Huge thank you for the contributions to: Dr Lindsay 'grammar' Kay, Dr Katie Pierce, Dr Richard Skelton, Dr Rachael Hornsby, Dr Rachel Lyons and Jade Charelson for their professional insight, unwavering friendship, invaluable contribution and time. You really are the Waitrose of Psychologists (quality wise, not overpriced!).

Thank you to all my family and friends who have endured numerous versions of these books and for their support during the periods in which I was very ill and gained tenacity from believing I could make something good come out of it all.

To Erin and Drew for being excellent guinea pigs and the source of great inspiration. To Owen for being a friend to me at 13 and 35 with admittedly slightly improved cooking skills. To Dianne Davies for her experience, support and knowledge of the area which helped more than you could know.

A huge thank you to Tim Watson for your supervision, guidance and support. You have helped me realise my potential when I couldn't see it in myself. You are an excellent critical friend, fountain of knowledge and all round lovely person!

Thanks to Catherine Hicks, my illustrator, the gin to my tonic! Perhaps in finding each other we made two slightly broken people whole.

To all my Zebra friends and those who have overcome adversity, keep going. Big up to Ellie Taylor for representing the herd!

Thanks for my Dad for always believing in me and constantly filling my freezer and thanks to my big brother John, who annoyed me as a child and who has always been there for me as an adult.

To the Hickling family, I couldn't have wished to marry into a better family, your support love and acceptance of me as a Scouser is forever appreciated.

Thank you to Jonathan Merrett, the copy editor, for his patience and flexibility and to Leah Burton, my Editorial Assistant, for her help along the way.

Finally, a huge thank you to Gillian Steadman, my Senior Production Editor, who is the yin to my yang. Couldn't have done this without you!

Introduction to the Resource Pack

This book is for the parents/carers and professionals supporting children who may be experiencing difficulties associated with depression. This resource has been created to:

- raise awareness
- explore the presentation, frequency and potential sources of support around a specific issue
- explain and find a common language to use around an issue to those experiencing it and those around them
- create empathy and help to normalise behaviours and feelings
- help children make sense of their feelings
- provide some strategies that may offer immediate help and support to children
- signpost when appropriate.

WHO IS THIS BOOK FOR?

This book was written with children with depression in mind and it is hoped they will relate to the thoughts, feelings, behaviours and experiences of Matilda. However, children with a range of needs may benefit from the story, and particularly if they experience any of the following:

- low and changeable mood
- recovery after a difficult experience
- recovery after a period of illness
- recovery from chemotherapy
- feelings of loss
- difficulty asking for help
- issues around body image/media pressures and comparison.

WHAT IS DEPRESSION?

Depression is more than just feeling sad. Depression invades all areas of a child's thinking, resulting in persistent negative thoughts about themselves and the future, which impact on

Copyright material from Dr Louise Lightfoot (2020), *Supporting Children with Depression to Understand and Celebrate Difference*, Routledge.

their ability to engage with people of activities. Depression affects up to 10% of all children, with 3% of children estimated to experience persistent depression.[1]

Behaviours that are typically associated with depression in children include:

- lack of enjoyment from previously enjoyed activities/relationships
- low energy or mood
- being easily irritable
- appearing overly sensitive to criticism/failure
- making overly negative predictions and comments about themselves
- difficulty concentrating and maintaining focus on activities
- have little interest in food or overeat
- difficulties with sleep and daily routines
- positioning of items/excessive neatness
- need for symmetry or 'exactness'
- repeating tasks or actions.

Someone with depression might have thoughts like . . .

I feel useless

I can't do things I normally do

I don't enjoy things I normally enjoy

No one would miss me if I wasn't around

I am not good at anything

I can't remember a time when I didn't feel like this

I will always feel like this.

1 https://adaa.org/living-with-anxiety/children/anxiety-and-depression

Copyright material from Dr Louise Lightfoot (2020), *Supporting Children with Depression to Understand and Celebrate Difference*, Routledge.

SUPPORTING CHILDREN IN THE CLASSROOM

Depression and low mood can present in a variety of ways in the classroom and can have a significant impact on a child's ability to engage with learning. Be mindful of the following signs that may suggest a child is experiencing low mood (this list is not exhaustive and should not be used as diagnostic criteria):

- difficulties in concentration
- isolation from peer group
- appearing upset or tearful with no apparent cause
- little interest or pleasure in doing things
- appearing tired or having low energy
- poor appetite or overeating
- moving or speaking really slowly or being fidgety and restless
- self-negating comments
- lack of self-care
- generally disinterested, i.e. a 'not-caring' attitude
- any significant changes in behaviour.

If you suspect a child in your class may be experiencing low mood, the first step would be to talk to them. Often, there is a reason a child is experiencing low mood and so our priority is to ensure that the child feels safe enough to share what is going on for them. Sometimes we need to make a number of adjustments to our classroom environment and practice to support the child, these might include:

Whole school level

- promote inclusion by focusing on wellbeing at the whole school level e.g. Starting each morning with emotion check-in or sharing time.
- create an environment that is open to *all* emotions i.e. 'it's okay not to be okay'.
- ensure the child has a key adult/s that they can go and feel safe to talk to.
- provide a safe space for the child to go when things feel too much.
- build in allocated time for the child to share their thoughts and feelings each day. Exposure to others' negative emotions and experiences can help them in feeling 'normal' and validated.

Copyright material from Dr Louise Lightfoot (2020), *Supporting Children with Depression to Understand and Celebrate Difference*, Routledge.

Class level

- Keep open-minded around academic expectations each day/lesson – are they ready to learn yet?
- Have a plan in place for when the child isn't ready to learn. What can we put in place to minimise gaps in learning?
- Look for the exceptions; when are the moments when they experience joy and motivation? What was happening? What were *you* doing? How can we make more of this happen?
- Take a strengths-based approach. What are their character strengths? How can we recognise and promote these each day?
- Work on building a good relationship with the child, getting to know who they are and what's important to them – build this into their school day.
- *Accept* the child for who they are and how they feel; validate their emotions rather than trying to change them.
- Think about the child's social world. Social connectedness can be a crucial aspect of our wellbeing. Rule out any bullying. Is some structured work needed to build some quality relationships for this child?
- Have you consulted with any outside agencies, i.e. an Educational Psychologist, for individualised advice?

SUPPORT FOR PARENTS

Parents want their child to feel better and want to remove the negative feelings that they are experiencing. Often this is done through reassurance, that things will get better of that things aren't that bad. This is especially true for depression where the young person's views perceptions are often not accurate. It can feel frightening to acknowledge the level of difficulty that a young person is experiencing, but in doing so, parents let their child see that they are listening to them and that they understand how difficult things feel. Emotional validation is much more supportive that reassurance because it values the young person and does not dismiss how they are feeling. Emotional validation involves listening to the underlying feeling that the young person is expressing, then feeding it back to them. It does not involve telling them that things will get better or giving advice at that time. Typical responses:

Child: 'Everything is horrible, I hate my life.'

Adult: 'Don't worry, things will get better', could be replaced with 'I understand that things feel really difficult at the moment'.

Copyright material from Dr Louise Lightfoot (2020), *Supporting Children with Depression to Understand and Celebrate Difference*, Routledge.

Child: 'This work is too difficult, I can't do it.'

Adult: 'Don't worry, just do as much as you can', could be replaced with 'It can feel scary at the start of something new; let me start this with you'.

TREATMENT

- CBT (Cognitive Behavioural Therapy) a form of 'talking therapy' has been shown to be very effective in the treatment of OCD. CBT helps people understand how thoughts, feelings and behaviours are linked, so they are better able to deal with upsetting thoughts and feelings. This approach can be adapted to meet the needs of young children, to older teenagers.
- Medication may also be offered; usually anti-depressant medications (Selective Serotonin Reuptake Inhibitors – SSRI) which may help reduce anxiety so as to better engage with CBT. Having a discussion about the pros and cons of such medication, and the potential side effects with your General Practitioner (GP) is important (the NICE Guidelines are available online and provide national guidance for England and Wales on the appropriate treatment and care of people with OCD, based on the best available evidence).
- EMDR (Eye Movement Desensitization and Reprocessing) is a psychotherapy that enables people to heal from the symptoms and emotional distress which have experienced. The therapy emphasises that the mind can in fact heal from psychological trauma much as the body recovers from physical trauma. The therapy looks to help you properly process these traumatic memories, reducing their impact and helping you develop healthy coping mechanisms. This is done through an eight-phase approach to address the past, present, and future aspects of a stored memory. This involves recalling distressing events while receiving 'bilateral sensory input', including side to side eye movements, hand tapping and auditory tones. It can be useful when dealing with a difficult event, anxiety or severe depression.
- Counselling is a way of talking and helping people to explore and think about things that may be worrying them, it also aids people if they are not sure what to do by giving them some time to think through possible ideas. An essential aspect of counselling is that the counsellors will not judge, criticise, interrogate or make decisions for the person they are seeing. Their aim is to listen, support and help people to decide what will work for them. There are different types of counselling and different styles and counsellors may be best suited for specific situation and for certain personality types.

SUPPORTING CHILDREN ON AN INDIVIDUAL LEVEL

It is important to be patient and empathic when supporting children who struggle with depression type behaviours. What may seem insignificant to an adult may be the cause of

Copyright material from Dr Louise Lightfoot (2020), *Supporting Children with Depression to Understand and Celebrate Difference*, Routledge.

great upset for the child. The following general approaches may be useful when supporting children and when working through the worksheets and resources provided.

Assessing the needs of each individual child and working safely within these limits is crucial. For some children, simply reading about a character that displays similar behaviours can have a positive impact in 'normalising' their behaviours and feelings. The activities in the resource pack are designed in such a way that the activities early on in the pack are not emotionally demanding and are designed to be fun and engaging and to consolidate their understanding of the story. During these activities the children are asked to focus on and consider the characters behaviours and feelings rather than their own. As the pack progresses, the child is expected to relate their own thoughts, feelings and behaviours to that of the characters therefore gaining insight into their own needs. Finally, the child is encouraged to consider and develop coping strategies which may relieve life their mood and support them to manage their behaviour. It is important that each child works at their own pace and is supported by a skilled adult who is able to assess the child's needs, limits and have plans as to how to help the child manage uncomfortable feelings resulting from 1:1 work. It is good practice to:

- Let the child set the pace.
- Work in a non-judgemental manner and refrain from interpreting pictures and content unless suitably qualified.
- Recognise that every child is different and will have different needs and interests. It is important to modify your approach depending on the age (chronological and developmental) ethnicity and relevant social/economic factors of the child.
- It is useful to consider each child's individual learning style, literacy and cognitive abilities as well as their emotional literacy. Some children do not enjoy reading/writing and may be reluctant to engage in what may be perceived as 'work'. This resource pack has been designed to engage particularly creative or active children through craft based/practical activities.
- It may be useful to start and end a session with 'problem-free talk' which includes activities that can be used to help the adult build rapport with the child and discover what is important to them.
- Do not let the activities you choose be restricted by the child's age. Some teenagers will enjoy what seems like 'childish' activities (e.g. dot to dot) while some younger children may be more able. It is always useful to start work with an activity that is non-threatening and well within their capabilities to build confidence and support the child to feel safe.

Copyright material from Dr Louise Lightfoot (2020), *Supporting Children with Depression to Understand and Celebrate Difference*, Routledge.

- It is useful to consider the role of the child's existing support network (home life and within school) and to collaborate with such persons in order to reinforce and advance the work taking place within sessions.
- It is important to come to sessions prepared with a back-up plan and to get to know if a child has a known interest, to include this at the end of a session or if a session becomes difficult or if the child is not easily engaged.
- It is important to reflect on (and if available, have supervision with a trained professional) as to the progress of any 1:1 work and to tailor your approaches accordingly.
- It is good practice to bring the child's earlier work to subsequent sessions so that you can refer back to it, chart progress and praise/show value in the work achieved.
- It is useful for most children to know when sessions are happening, what they will entail and how long they will last. It is particularly important for children with anxiety and control issues to know in advance of sessions what is to be expected of them and for any change in a set timetable or cancellation to be shared with the child as soon as possible.

USEFUL LINKS

www.nhs.uk/conditions/stress-anxiety-depression/anxiety-in-children/

Young Minds: www.youngminds.org.uk 0808 802 5544 (parents/carers)

Child Line: www.childline.org.uk 0800 1111

Anxiety UK: www.anxietyuk.org.uk 08444 775 774

For parents/carers/professionals wishing to seek help for themselves: www.rubywax.net/frazzled-cafe.html

HELPFUL BOOKS

S. Hamil, *My Feeling Better Workbook: Help for Kids Who Are Sad and Depressed*

M. E. P. Seligman, *The Optimistic Child: Safeguarding Children Against Depression*

D. Serani, *Depression and Your Child: A Guide for Parents and Caregivers*

C. Kerr, *Rays of Calm* (Audio CD to develop relaxation skills)

The Margot Sunderland story books

Copyright material from Dr Louise Lightfoot (2020), *Supporting Children with Depression to Understand and Celebrate Difference*, Routledge.

Chapter 1

Feelings generator

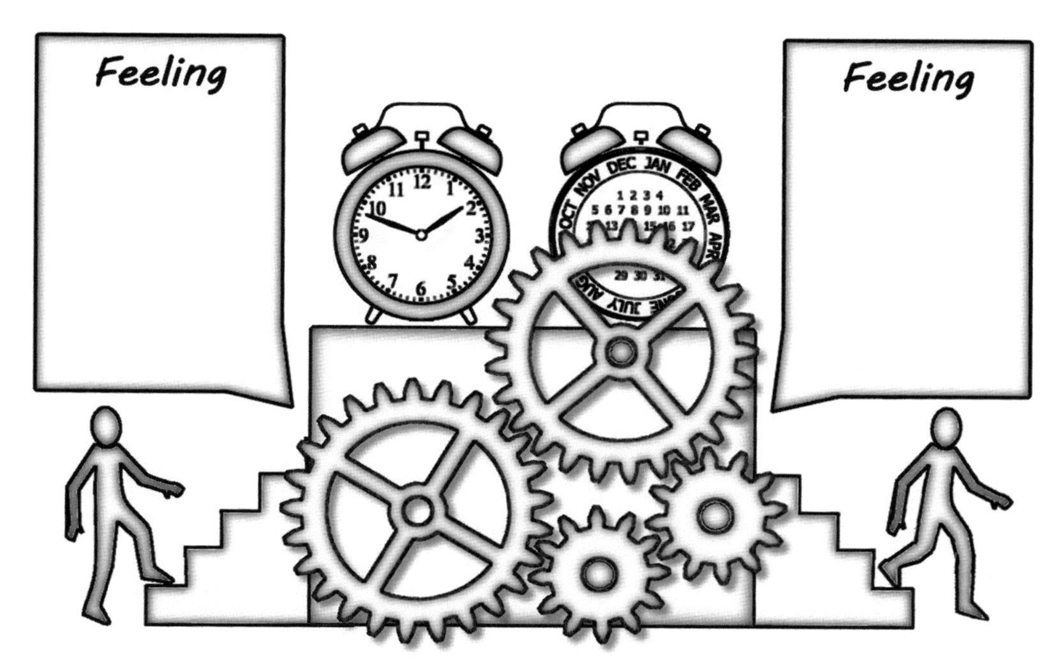

The Feelings Generator

The feelings generator can help us to understand the feelings that maybe causing our behaviour. There are often many different names used to describe the same feeling and this can make it tricky to understand and express how we are feeling.

Below is an example of how the feeling 'angry' can be described in different ways:

Angry = mad, grumpy, frustrated, annoyed, irritated, furious, cross, fuming, raging

Can you think of anymore?

Continue to find others names for the following feelings:

- Scared
- Anxious
- Happy
- Ashamed
- Proud
- Sad
- Bad

Do you notice anything about the terms? Do some seem stronger than others? Do some fit into more than one category? Having a big emotional vocabulary can help to express our feelings and needs to others.

Copyright material from Dr Louise Lightfoot (2020), *Supporting Children with Depression to Understand and Celebrate Difference*, Routledge.

Using the flash cards provided overleaf, write down the different feelings and see if, when you mix them all together, you are able to group these feelings back with the initial term. For example, all feelings related to angry would be placed under the 'angry' flash card.

Additional activities:

- Photocopy the flash cards so there are two sets of each feeling. Use these to play 'snap'. This helps to improve word recognition.
- Place the photocopied flash cards on a table in a random order paying close attention to the cards. Then turn them over and pick up two cards displaying the same feeling if you can remember where the cards are! Set aside each matched 'pair'. This can be played alone or with others. The person with the most pairs wins! This game improves memory and attention.
- Mix the cards up and use to play charades. Each person should pick a card and act out that feeling whilst the other players guess. This can be done in a pair or in teams. This is useful in supporting emotional intelligence and for recognising behaviours in ourselves and others.

Copyright material from Dr Louise Lightfoot (2020), *Supporting Children with Depression to Understand and Celebrate Difference*, Routledge.

Copyright material from Dr Louise Lightfoot (2020), *Supporting Children with Depression to Understand and Celebrate Difference*, Routledge.

Chapter 2

Sympathy or empathy

When someone is upset or seems sad there is often is an urge to be nice to that person and to want to make them feel better. This can be done in several ways, one of them involves being sympathetic to that person and one involves being empathetic (or showing empathy) – but what is the difference?

Sympathy is looking at someone's situation and feeling bad for them or feeling emotions of pity and sadness but looking at the situation from a distance. It is by no means bad to feel sympathy for others and many good things happen because people are sympathetic. It is, however, different from empathy as there is a distance or a barrier that remains – I'm looking *at* you not *with* you.

Empathy, however, is about looking at someone's situation from their perspective and trying to put yourself in their shoes. Empathy involves closing the distance between you and the person you are empathising with and the narrowing of this distance forges connection.

Think about these two scenarios:

Owen comes across Matilda and notices her feathers are gone and she is cold. He flies away and returns giving her a blanket. He flies away.

Owen comes across Matilda and notices her feathers are gone and she is cold. He sits down by her side and does not leave until she is well.

They are both kind acts but in which one is Owen showing *sympathy* and in which one is he showing *empathy*? If you had been Matilda, which would have preferred?

Copyright material from Dr Louise Lightfoot (2020), *Supporting Children with Depression to Understand and Celebrate Difference*, Routledge.

Exercise: Can you think of times you have shown empathy and sympathy and what was the difference?

When you have experienced empathy or sympathy which felt better?

What kinds of ways/phrases or actions could you offer to someone in the future to show empathy?

Copyright material from Dr Louise Lightfoot (2020), *Supporting Children with Depression to Understand and Celebrate Difference*, Routledge.

Chapter 3

Using puppets and play to explore emotions

Puppets can be a great way to engage children in play as they are not only fun but give children a feeling of distance from what they might feel comfortable saying and what the puppet is able to say on their behalf. You might find that a child will reveal more when talking 'through a puppet' that when asked directly. It should also be noted that some children use puppets to simply play and use their imagination.

HOW TO MAKE A PUPPET

Materials needed:

Paper towel holders or toilet paper cardboard holder

Wiggly eyes

Wool

Colourful paper

Paint

Scissors

Blue tack

Glue.

Directions:

- Cover the toilet or paper towel cardboard holder with coloured paper or paint. You may want to use different colours for the face, body and clothing.
- Use the 'emotion tracker' to make different facial expressions that can be switched on and off using blue tack as appropriate
- Choose wool to make the hair and glue it on the top of the paper towel holder/toilet paper holder.
- Decorate the puppet! This can be done by drawing or painting on clothes, or adding stickers.
- A large lollipop stick can be added at the base of the puppet so it can be held up by the child.

Puppets can be used in various ways. These include:

- To engage shy or reluctant children to speak out.
- To enact past experience or confrontations and to replay them after reflection and to act out 'what could' have been done differently.

Copyright material from Dr Louise Lightfoot (2020), *Supporting Children with Depression to Understand and Celebrate Difference*, Routledge.

- To 'practice' difficult situations with children so they can rely on a series of 'scripts' to deal with difficult or novel situations. Not only are 'scripts' useful in helping the child to act appropriately in the moment but merely practicing the scripts can often alleviate anxiety.

For example, when a child asks 'what's wrong with you?' a script might be:

'I find new situations and change hard to deal with. I might need some help at these times. Can I help you in anyway?'

It can be useful to practice what can be unhelpful comments, although they might be said with good intentions.

For example when a child reports 'feeling sad' an unsuitable script might be:

'Don't be silly, what do you have to sad about, it's your birthday next week and you'll gets lots of presents, you should be very happy, some children don't get any presents!'

It can, therefore, be useful to build empathy and understanding not only with those experiencing difficulties, but those around them. When we are feeling emotionally vulnerable, what people say can have more impact than usual. It is therefore important to be sensitive and considerate with language and with actions and to validate and empathise with those suffering with poor mental health.

Copyright material from Dr Louise Lightfoot (2020), *Supporting Children with Depression to Understand and Celebrate Difference*, Routledge.

Chapter 4

True or false

Materials needed: Game cards

Purpose: Often children with difficulties around low or changeable mood may experience feelings of being different and feeling 'strange', and may struggle relate to their peers. Using a quiz is a useful way to dismiss myths and to instil positive and accurate information about depression and mental health. It is a fun way of reflecting back to the child that their feelings are normal and they are valued.

Instructions: Copy the statements below onto the game cards and shuffle them. Ask the player to choose a card and then state whether the comment is true or false. Discuss the answers. If the answer is correct place the card on the table and form a pile. If wrong, do the same with a different pile. The aim is to achieve more true answers than false.

TRUE STATEMENTS ABOUT DEPRESSION

Sometimes I don't know how I feel

Being asked what is wrong all the time can make me feel worse

When I hide away is when I might need contact the most

I am trying to get better

I still care about you, even if I don't show it

Sometimes I care more about other people than I do about myself

There are days I cannot get out of bed, not matter how much I try

Sometimes doing something small, like having a shower, feels like a big achievement

Some days I don't feel anything and some days I feel everything

If you see me out and about that doesn't mean I am better; I am very good at hiding how I really feel

I'm scared I will always feel this way

FALSE STATEMENTS ABOUT DEPRESSION

One in ten people will experience mental health issues (actually one in four)

People who experience mental illness often turn violent (more likely to be the victim)

You can catch depression

Copyright material from Dr Louise Lightfoot (2020), *Supporting Children with Depression to Understand and Celebrate Difference*, Routledge.

If I have depression my children will have depression (there is a genetic link but this is not definite)

Depression isn't a real illness

Everyone gets depressed, everyone gets sad sometimes

Depression only affects women

Depression affects adults not children

Antidepressants change your personality

Outcome: Using these cards not only gives child the opportunity to feel normal but gives them a clear sense of facts around the issue. This is likely to ground the child and aid understanding. Having a shared understanding between peers, adults and those suffering can be invaluable in making progress.

Copyright material from Dr Louise Lightfoot (2020), *Supporting Children with Depression to Understand and Celebrate Difference*, Routledge.

Chapter 5

Miracle questions

Imagine you went to sleep you and all the difficult feelings you had went away. When you woke up . . .

- What would it be like?
- Who would be there?
- How would your day start?
- What would happen next?
- What else . . .?
- What you are doing?

Draw or discuss.

Copyright material from Dr Louise Lightfoot (2020), *Supporting Children with Depression to Understand and Celebrate Difference*, Routledge.

Chapter 6

Colour your feelings

- Pick colours that represent different emotions.
- Use colours to represent how you might feel in different situations.
- Where do you feel things in your body?

Copyright material from Dr Louise Lightfoot (2020), *Supporting Children with Depression to Understand and Celebrate Difference*, Routledge.

Chapter 7

Compliment cards, part 1

Materials needed: Paper or note cards and pen.

Purpose: Often children with difficulties around control and anxiety suffer with low self-esteem. They may experience feelings of being different and feeling 'strange' and may struggle relate to their peers. Using compliment cards is a way of reflecting back to the child their strengths and enabling them to see how many people value them.

Instructions: Give the compliment cards to significant adults (and when appropriate other children) in the child's life (for example, teachers, parents, siblings, lunch time supervisors) and ask them to write a compliment about them. The compliment may relate to their personal qualities, an academic subject they engage well with or a specific talent or skill they have. The adult then reads the compliment to the child and they are asked to guess who wrote that compliment about them. The compliment cards game is played regularly or until the child can correctly identify the author of the compliment.

Outcome: Using these cards not only gives child the opportunity to feel appreciated and valued but they are able to see the range of people available to them. It might be that one particular feature appears in many of the compliment cards and this can be identified as a particular strength which is confirmed by many people making this more likely to be accepted. If a variety of different compliments are offered by those taking part, this can be used to show the child just how many good qualities they have. Asking the child to 'guess' who the compliments are from rather than just being asked to read them, not only makes the activity more fun but also makes the process more comfortable for children who may struggle to receive direct compliments due to poor self-esteem. Placing the focus on guessing the source of the compliment changes the focus of the game initially whilst continuing to allow the child to hear the compliments. The repetition of this game is designed to ensure that the child hears the compliments over and over, supporting the child to believe them and increasing self-esteem.

Copyright material from Dr Louise Lightfoot (2020), *Supporting Children with Depression to Understand and Celebrate Difference*, Routledge.

Chapter 8

Compliment cards, part 2

Materials needed: Paper or note cards and pen.

Purpose: Often children with difficulties with control and feel there is a 'right' way of doing things. The right way is typically theirs! Subsequently they may struggle to see things from the perspective of others or to value views when they are in opposition to their own. This may lead them to experience feelings of being different or 'strange' and they may not relate well to their peers. Working with the child to create compliment cards is a way of encouraging empathy, supporting the child to see good qualities in others and fostering flexible thinking.

Instructions: Give the child blank compliment cards and ask them to write down compliments about significant adults (and when appropriate other children) in their life (for example, teachers, parents, siblings, lunch time supervisors). The compliments may relate to their personal qualities or a specific talent or skill they have. If the child is confident enough, they can be supported to read the compliment to the relevant person along with a compliment about someone else. The child then asks the person to identify which compliment relates to them. If they are not confident enough to do this, they can keep the collection of cards which can be reviewed to remind the child that we all have different strengths.

Outcome: The participants are not only given the opportunity to identify good qualities in others but are then able to practice sharing this appreciation with others. This allows the child not only to improve their social skills but encourages them to see the diversity in people and to appreciate their skills. It is hoped that through such an activity the child can, through appreciating others, learn to appreciate themselves and their special skills and qualities.

Copyright material from Dr Louise Lightfoot (2020), *Supporting Children with Depression to Understand and Celebrate Difference*, Routledge.

Chapter 9

Remember a time

- Remember a time when you didn't have these feelings . . .
- What was that like and what were you doing?
- Draw or describe . . .

Copyright material from Dr Louise Lightfoot (2020), *Supporting Children with Depression to Understand and Celebrate Difference*, Routledge.

Chapter 10

Always, never, everybody

When someone is feeling low it can be hard not to generalise negative feelings and to use language that supports staying in a negative frame of mind. Ask them to try and spot when they use phrases like:

- always,
- everybody,
- nobody,
- everywhere,
- no one,
- always,
- never,

and to write them down, it might be a useful idea to collect these 'statements' in a jar for reference as an aid to monitor progress. It may also be helpful to ask the child to try and think of a different way of phrasing it.

Tracking the use of such language can be a useful way of indicating good and bad days and showing progress.

Copyright material from Dr Louise Lightfoot (2020), *Supporting Children with Depression to Understand and Celebrate Difference*, Routledge.

Chapter 11

Feelings sorter

Often our behaviour gives us clues about how we are feeling deep down. Sometimes we might act angry when we are actually feeling worried. Use the feeling sorter to enter 'in' a behaviour and try to figure out what the 'underlying' feeling might be.

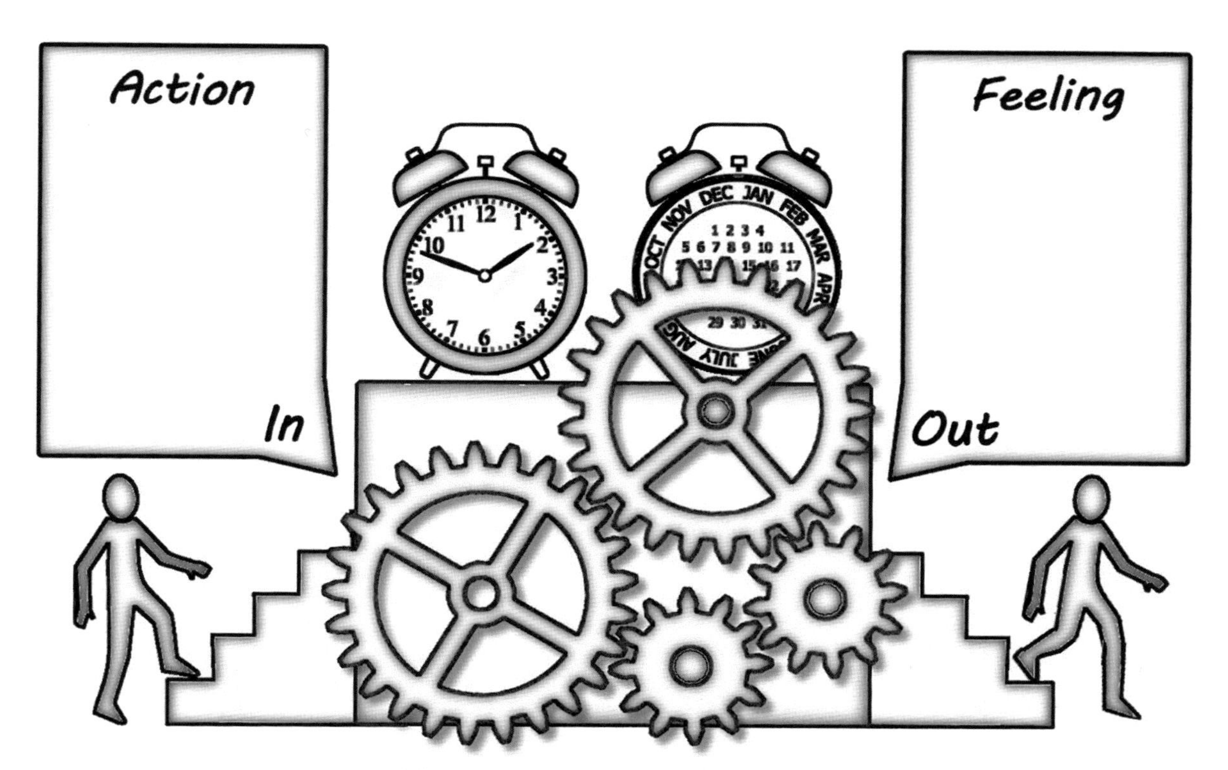

Copyright material from Dr Louise Lightfoot (2020), *Supporting Children with Depression to Understand and Celebrate Difference*, Routledge.

Chapter 12

The bridge to success

Bridge to Success

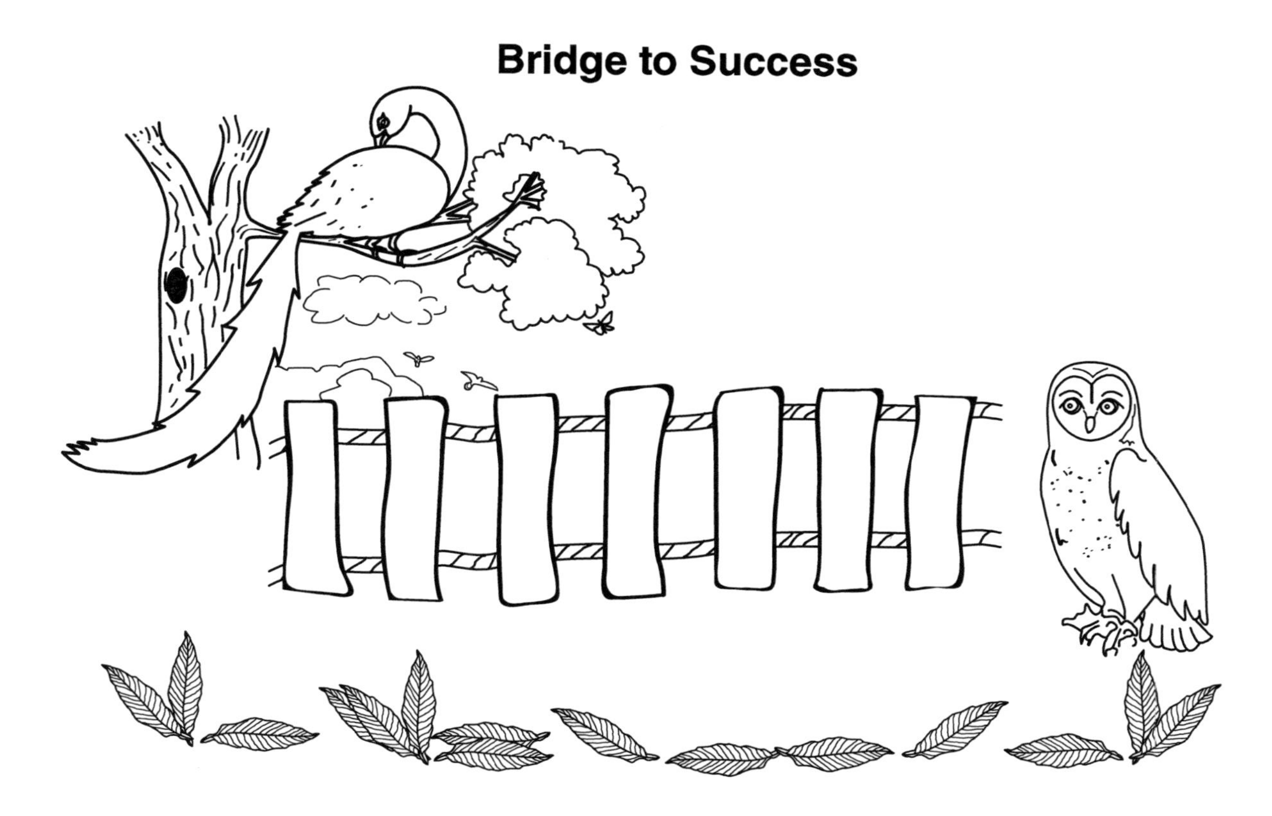

This game helps children to identify elements of the child's life that they would like to succeed in and helps them to plan (with the help of metaphor) a course of action that will help them move forward.

In all real-life situations there are forces and circumstances that impact either positively or negatively on any given outcome. This game helps the child the look at the impact of outside influences be it positive it or negative.

The bridge to success represents positive steps that need to be taken by the child in order to get to the other side or the desired changes. This may involve engaging in a particular behaviour e.g. attending school, refraining from a particular behaviour e.g. abusing drugs, and seeking support for example school counsellor. These would all constitute 'steps' across the bridge.

'Threats' to achieving these goals should be identified to allow the person the best possible chance of tackling and avoiding such threats. Threats may include: peer pressure, addiction and their own self-belief.

Each threat and step should be discussed and planned for with a supportive adult to increase the likelihood of achieving their goals, and giving them the tools and the confidence they need to successfully cross the bridge.

Copyright material from Dr Louise Lightfoot (2020), *Supporting Children with Depression to Understand and Celebrate Difference*, Routledge.

Chapter 13

Silver Matilda's Activity Book

Silver Matilda's Activity Book

Copyright material from Dr Louise Lightfoot (2020), *Supporting Children with Depression to Understand and Celebrate Difference*, Routledge.

Colour In

Silver Matilda

Copyright material from Dr Louise Lightfoot (2020), *Supporting Children with Depression to Understand and Celebrate Difference*, Routledge.

Matilda's Dot-to-Dot

Join the dots to complete the picture.
You can colour it in if you like.

Copyright material from Dr Louise Lightfoot (2020), *Supporting Children with Depression to Understand and Celebrate Difference*, Routledge.

Silver Matilda is soaring through the sky.

Which cloud did she start from - A, B, C or D?

Copyright material from Dr Louise Lightfoot (2020), *Supporting Children with Depression to Understand and Celebrate Difference*, Routledge.

Silver Matilda's Crossword

Clues Across :

2: Precious stones do this (7)
3: A night bird (3)
4: Someone you like and want to spend time with (6)
6: When a river or stream flows over a cliff (9)
8: Birds fly with these (5)
10: The sun does this (5)
11: Precious stones (8)
13: shiny yellow metal (4)
15: All by yourself (5)
16: What the owl did for Matilda (6)

Clues Down:

1: The name of the bird (7)
4: Birds are covered with these. (8)
5: Very, very sad (9)
7: Falls from the sky in winter (4)
9: Bright, glowing (7)
11: A precious metal in Matilda's name (6)
13: Unhappy (3)

Copyright material from Dr Louise Lightfoot (2020), *Supporting Children with Depression to Understand and Celebrate Difference*, Routledge.

Clues Across :

2: Precious stones do this (7)
3: A night bird (3)
4: Someone you like and want to spend time with (6)
6: When a river or stream flows over a cliff (9)
8: Birds fly with these (5)
10: The sun does this (5)
11: Precious stones (8)
13: shiny yellow metal (4)
15: All by yourself (5)
16: What the owl did for Matilda (6)

Clues Down:

1: The name of the bird (7)
4: Birds are covered with these. (8)
5: Very, very sad (9)
7: Falls from the sky in winter (4)
9: Bright, glowing (7)
11: A precious metal in Matilda's name (6)
13: Unhappy (3)

Copyright material from Dr Louise Lightfoot (2020), *Supporting Children with Depression to Understand and Celebrate Difference*, Routledge.

Show Matilda the way through the maze to her friend the owl.

Copyright material from Dr Louise Lightfoot (2020), *Supporting Children with Depression to Understand and Celebrate Difference*, Routledge.

Silver Matilda's Word Search

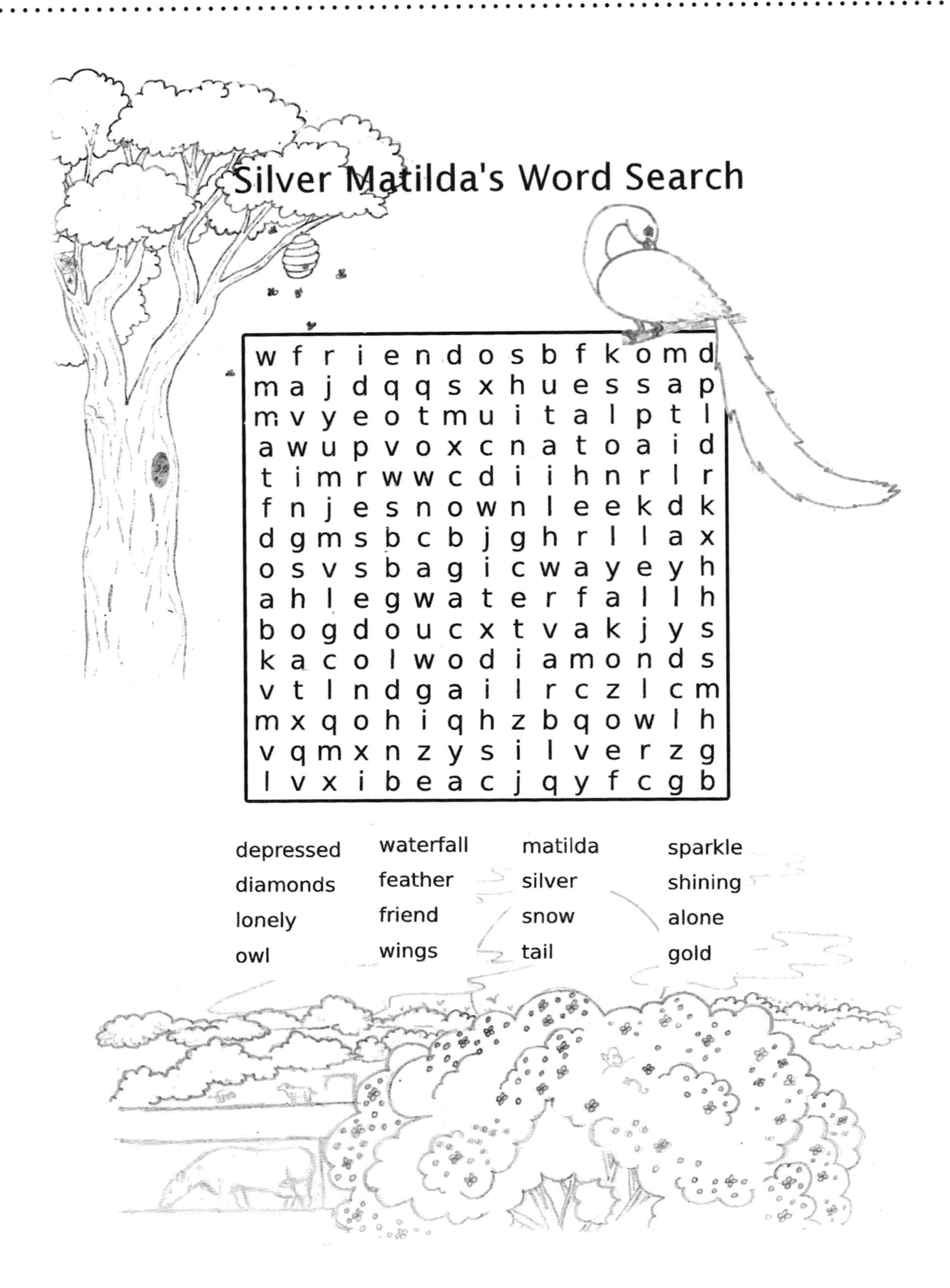

depressed	waterfall	matilda	sparkle
diamonds	feather	silver	shining
lonely	friend	snow	alone
owl	wings	tail	gold

Copyright material from Dr Louise Lightfoot (2020), *Supporting Children with Depression to Understand and Celebrate Difference*, Routledge.

There are ten differences between these two pictures.
Can you find them all?

Copyright material from Dr Louise Lightfoot (2020), *Supporting Children with Depression to Understand and Celebrate Difference*, Routledge.

The owl did not leave Matilda's side. Why do you think this was important? Can you think of ways in which you could help someone you cared for feel valued and let them know you were thinking of them?

Copyright material from Dr Louise Lightfoot (2020), *Supporting Children with Depression to Understand and Celebrate Difference*, Routledge.

Silver Matilda is soaring through the sky.
Which cloud did she start from - A, B, C or D?

Answers

Copyright material from Dr Louise Lightfoot (2020), *Supporting Children with Depression to Understand and Celebrate Difference*, Routledge.

Silver Matilda's Crossword

ANSWERS

Clues Across :

2: Precious stones do this (7)
3: A night bird (3)
4: Someone you like and want to spend time with (6)
6: When a river or stream flows over a cliff (9)
8: Birds fly with these (5)
10: The sun does this (5)
11: Precious stones (8)
13: shiny yellow metal (4)
15: All by yourself (5)
16: What the owl did for Matilda (6)

Clues Down:

1: The name of the bird (7)
4: Birds are covered with these. (8)
5: Very, very sad (9)
7: Falls from the sky in winter (4)
9: Bright, glowing (7)
11: A precious metal in Matilda's name (6)
13: Unhappy (3)

Copyright material from Dr Louise Lightfoot (2020), *Supporting Children with Depression to Understand and Celebrate Difference*, Routledge.

Show Matilda the way through the maze to her friend the owl.

ANSWER

Copyright material from Dr Louise Lightfoot (2020), *Supporting Children with Depression to Understand and Celebrate Difference*, Routledge.

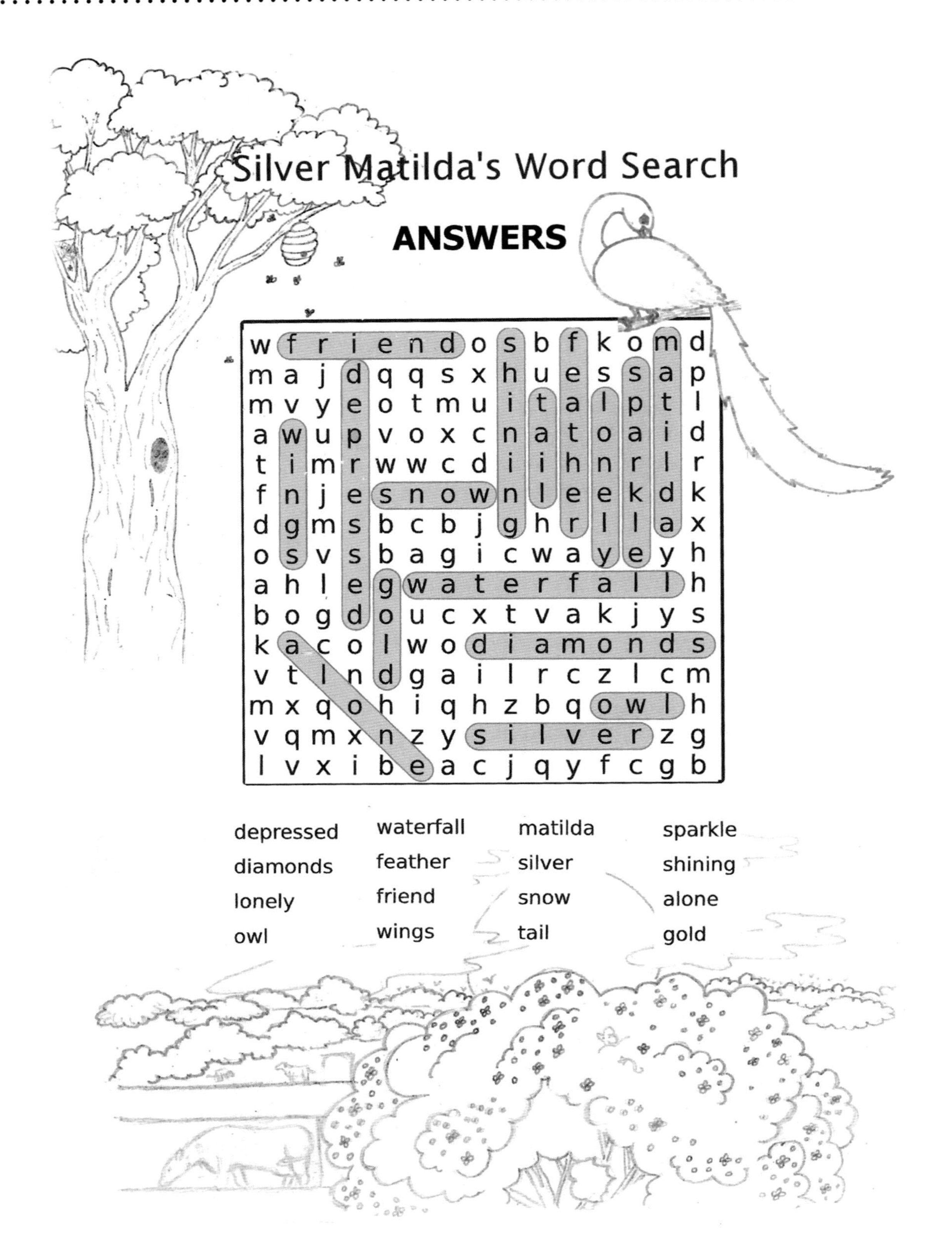

Copyright material from Dr Louise Lightfoot (2020), *Supporting Children with Depression to Understand and Celebrate Difference*, Routledge.

There are ten differences between these two pictures.

ANSWERS

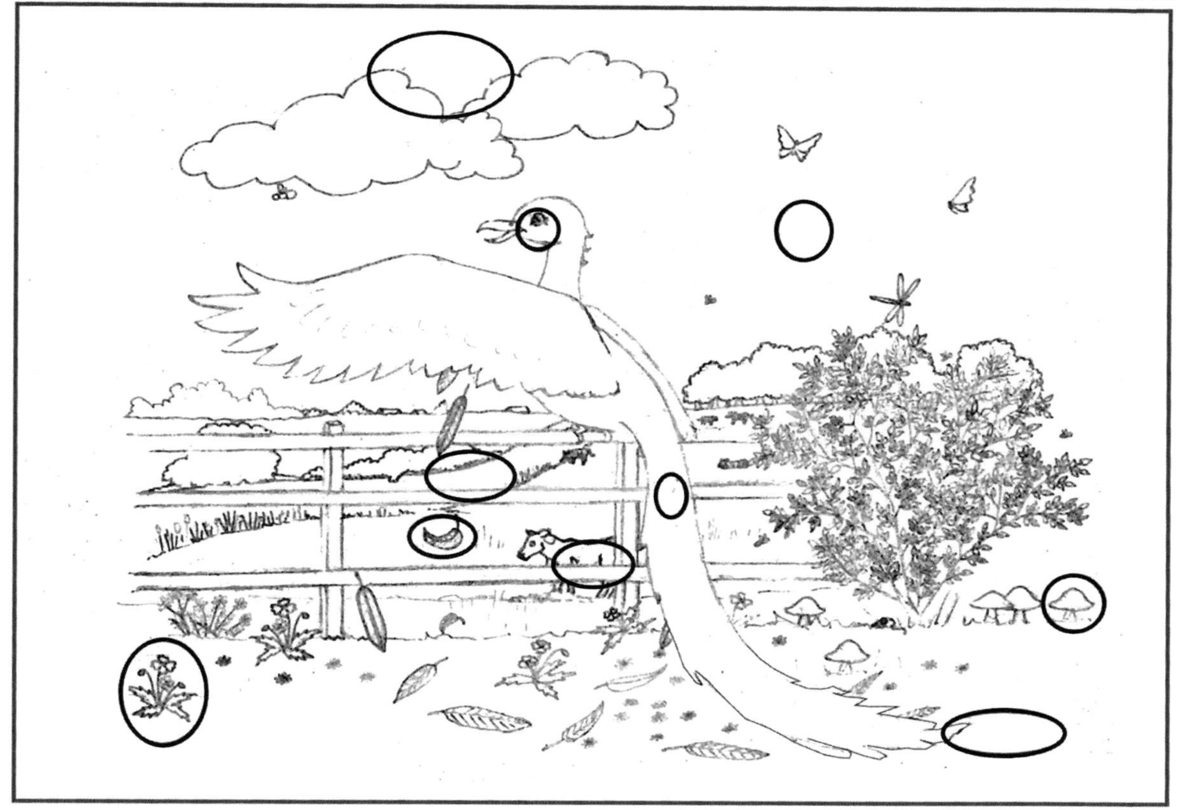

Copyright material from Dr Louise Lightfoot (2020), *Supporting Children with Depression to Understand and Celebrate Difference*, Routledge.

Chapter 14

Silver Matilda's Board Game

NOTES AND ADVICE WHEN PLAYING THE BOARD GAME.

The questions are designed to vary in terms of difficulty to allow some children answer some questions unaided. This can be useful not only in consolidating the story but maintaining or improving confidence.

More complicated questions are included which may be answered by older or more able children and they may do so unaided but others may require discussion and support from supportive adults. It may be that discussing and talking through the question is enough to generate a sufficient answer or it might be that the child will have to refer back to the book to find the answer. Either method is acceptable as the goal is to acquire a better understanding of the narrative and underlying themes of the book. It is hoped that by truly understanding the story, its characters, their behaviour, and how that impacts on them and others, they will be able to apply and relate the thoughts, feelings and emotions of the characters and their situations to their own lives and struggles. Reading a book about others experiencing similar difficulties not only normalises their thoughts feelings and actions but opens a dialogue around these issues and helps them to formulate plans and to think of ways to cope and seek support in their own life.

Please copy the questions below onto the game cards overleaf, the game cards should then be split 50/50 across the two shaded/coloured boxes on the game board. These form the basis of the game and all players should start on Silver Matilda. A colour version of this game is available online as an eResource.

QUESTIONS FOR SILVER MATILDA'S BOARD GAME

Matilda loses what? (move 2 spaces)

Owen helped how? (move 3 spaces)

Matilda is embarrassed why? (move 3 spaces)

How long did Owen stay with Matilda for? (move 3 spaces)

Did Matilda ask for help how? (move 1 spaces)

Why do you think Owen stayed with Matilda? (move 3 spaces)

Was Matilda is happy in the end? Why? (move 3 spaces)

How did Owen help Matilda? (move 3 spaces)

What did Matilda need to help her recover? (move 2 spaces)

What type of creature is Matilda? (move 1 space)

What type of creature is Owen? (move 1 space)

Copyright material from Dr Louise Lightfoot (2020), *Supporting Children with Depression to Understand and Celebrate Difference*, Routledge.

What colour is Matilda in the beginning of the book? (move 1 space)

What colour is Matilda at the end of the book? (move 2 spaces)

How would you describe Matilda before she felt sad? (move 3 space)

What did Matilda see when she opened her eyes for the first time? (move 2 spaces)

How did Matilda feel when she lost her feathers (move 3 spaces)

What did the Owen see when he looked at Matilda? (move 3 spaces)

What do you think Matilda learned from losing her feathers? (move 3 spaces).

Apart from losing her feathers how would we know Matilda was feeling sad? (move 3 spaces)

Name three words or phrases that describe Matilda before she felt sad (move 5 spaces)

Name three words or phrases that describe Matilda whilst she was feeling sad (move 5 spaces)

What was it about Owen that Matilda found helpful? (move 3 spaces)

Name another type of bird (move 1 space)

Do you think feelings last for ever or can they change? (move 3 spaces)

Do you think Matilda was stronger at the end of the story? Why? (move 3 spaces)

How do you think being there for Matilda made Owen feel? (move 3 spaces)

Do you think Owen being with Matilda help change her mood and help her feathers grow back? (move 3 spaces)

Can having a bad thing happen to us make us stronger? (move 2 spaces)

Copyright material from Dr Louise Lightfoot (2020), *Supporting Children with Depression to Understand and Celebrate Difference*, Routledge.

Copyright material from Dr Louise Lightfoot (2020), *Supporting Children with Depression to Understand and Celebrate Difference*, Routledge.

Copyright material from Dr Louise Lightfoot (2020), *Supporting Children with Depression to Understand and Celebrate Difference*, Routledge.

Chapter 15

What happens next?

- Draw, use crafts or continue to write the story.
- Do things turn out well for the characters?
- How has what has happened affected them?

Copyright material from Dr Louise Lightfoot (2020), *Supporting Children with Depression to Understand and Celebrate Difference*, Routledge.

Chapter 16

Alternate ending?

- Draw, use crafts or re-write the ending of Matilda's story.
- Do things still turn out well for the characters?
- What happens instead?

Copyright material from Dr Louise Lightfoot (2020), *Supporting Children with Depression to Understand and Celebrate Difference*, Routledge.